Souls Talk

Flying Out of Time

Dr. Fatema Omran

Copyright © 2020 by Dr. Fatema Omran

All rights reserved.

No part of this book may be reproduced in any form or by any electronic or mechanical means, including information storage and retrieval systems, without written permission from the author, except for the use of brief quotations in a book review.

ISBN: 978-0-578-56213-1

Author images by Rebecca Hurley Photography

All Poems Translated from Arabic to English by Dr. Nizar Sofani (except the Dedication, *Beautiful Wisconsin*, *Souls Talk*, *Whispering Voice*, *Syria Syria*, and *Life & Eternity*—all written by the author in English)

All paintings and images by the author

Some names and identifying details have been changed to protect the privacy of individuals.

To my mother Amira
For the compassionate soul within the heart, the light within the spirit
For the sun of my Life, Amira Afif

To every wounded, kind soul
When confusion and delusion in your life are cleared up by faith and courage. Your soul will rise freely in a world of eternity full of peace, love, and joy.
Remember.
Darkness is always followed by light.
Pain is always followed by joy.

CONTENTS

Life and Eternity	1
Whispering Voice	3
Souls Talk	7
Beautiful Wisconsin	11
Handcuff of Eggs	15
Lilli	19
Shereen and Domestic Violence	23
Flying Out of Time	29
Mistook the Address	37
I Declared My Defection	43
Syria Syria	47
Mother of the Martyr	51
Wheat Spikes	57
The Bread Loaf	61
Stop Attacking	65

FOREWORD

A journey between the Continents without paying attention to space, achieving the Journey in Time without using a machine, a stir of sensations and feelings through her homeland, and also that Big country, which we thank for opening their doors to give us shelter, and the power to keep making our dreams come true in peace.

That peace and inner freedom that allows us to enjoy the Divine gift.

The author claims that freedom, for her conquered; for those who still cry, from the daily suffering of pain, cheers loudly as a spokeswoman for the right of that child, that woman, that man assaulted by his fellow man, attracted by selfishness or spiritual blindness.

In poetry you move along with her from the bosom of a family that demands the kiss, the hug, the memory of the games during childhood, the most tender of memories among siblings, which one day were separated by an accumulation of water called Ocean, and lots of unusual ideas absurd among human beings.

In her book you can also feel the claim to the exile of those who were trapped and suffer every day, the pain of those who are no longer close, because they left to different dimensions.

When she mentions the state of Wisconsin, she manages to make a perfect painting of its four seasons, with its wonderful flora and fauna, its colorful autumn, its multitude of lakes and beautiful beings of heart and spirit who know each day to share the best and most precious of the human being: Love.

The book is an excellent proposal also to let the imagination fly and reflect on who we are and the beauty that surrounds us. The visceral pain that makes us doubt the Magnificent Work of our Creator, and at the same time makes us grow.

I think that through reading books like this, we are growing humanly every day in the simple, but deep knowledge of the answers to the basic existential questions: Who are we? Where do we come from? Where do we go?

—Dr. Perez Romano

IMPRESSIONS FROM THE EDITOR

The poems in this book show a woman of grace, courage, and conviction who is not afraid to show her generous and tender heart. They are a pleasure and privilege to read.

—ER

LIFE & ETERNITY

The purl of the river water tenderly tickles my soul
Pours softly all the peace and love I can ever look for
The dawn brings me the sunlight of the joyful life
The light of the day overwhelms my heart with pleasure and joy
These rays of happiness warm my world the perfect way. I ever aim
The soft wind ravaged my heart with the breeze of Ocean, rivers, and sea
The scent of spring flowers refreshes my soul with tenderness and hope
Yes, my love, here I am

Holding happily all the precious memories we had
Waiting for your endless love
So we can whisper together the poem we both shared in old times
Eternity kindly seals our two souls in one
Peace and love is all what eternity is about
Life is the birth of wonderful eternity in all times

Whispering Voice

*In this silent night
I heard this voice
Whispering tenderly
in my ears
Wake up, son
Wake up, son
Good morning, son
Good morning, son
Today is a new day
Today is a new life*

*I ignored this voice
Over and over
since I was tired
Tired and sad*

*The voice whispered again
Son, son
I heard your prayer
I felt your pain
I sense suffering
In your wounded soul
I saw tears in your helpless eyes
I saw you struggling
Day and night
Figuring out a way to make you survive
I touch fear in your heart
and blaming in your thoughts
Is there God?
Is there God?
Where is God?
Where is God?
Why is He not listening to me?
Why is He not answering me*

Like He always did in the past?
And here I am, my son
Here I am
Listening to you
As your heart asks
listen to me
Listen to me
Be patient, my son, with all your stressful life
I am here for you
as I was in the past and in all future time
Have faith in you
Have faith in me
We both are
two souls in one
We both soon
Can Open the door
To achieve your goals.
Your future goals

In this silent night
Your soul whispers softly to me
Help me, God
Help me, God
With peace and love
Like spring full trees
Green, pink, and white
I am refreshing your soul
Showering your path
With the knowledge you need
As well as mercy and love
Knowledge of life
Is the Path to joy
The path of learning, caring, and sharing
In every way you know

My son, my son
In this silent night
I am freeing you from all
Suffering and pain you ever had
Remember, my son
What you are facing in life
Is part of this life
Life will always be up and down
Joyful moment there
Painful moment there
Failure and success
Loss and gain
But at the end
Nothing lasts forever the same

Do not forget to pass this gift
The meaning of life
To whoever you meet
The gift of faith
The gift of joy
To all the ones who need or ask

Souls Talk

From Uncle Sam Land to the Syrian Land

A Dialogue Poem Between Brother & Sister

FATEMA:

I whispered softly your name, Mahmoud
Fearful of waking you up in the middle of the night

brother, brother
It has been a long long time

Since our childhood seeded in our hearts

Waking up the precious memories
hidden in the depth of our minds

My soul is flying freely over the oceans, seas, rivers
Mountains, valleys, and even hidden rocks

Trying to hug you as I always did in our childhood
Our golden time

Are you still there, my dear
In our beautiful yard house

Painting colors on a piece of glass like old times
Painting of horses racing happily in the land of God
Are you still there!!!
playing the same cheerful music
you shared kindly with us
Soft Music touched my soul with kindness and love
Helping me sleep deeply
in the hands of God
Fly me away
like a free bird
high, high in the blue sky

Where peace can draw
the rainbow colors
in the eyes of the wounded man

Are you still there!!
Where you taught me
how to swim
like a free dolphin
With his happy sounds
how to dive deeply
without fearing that I may die

Are you still there!!!
where all our precious memories
printed the colorful lines
of the story of mankind
Mankind where
caring, love, and peace
is all what is real life about ?!
I see my soul wipes
Your beautiful blue eyes
Blue eyes crying sadly on Syria
The land of peace and love
I sense my soul
hugging you
As I used to do strongly
when I was I a little girl
fearful of losing
her secure land!???

MAHMOUD:

I caught your soul
roaming over my soul

take me back
to a lovely memories and precious time...
Children were together getting older
Swimming, reading, drawing
And listening to music
Favorite Music of all mankind
Watching happily, Jasmine's flowers
Jasmine flowers,
flowers of peace, mercy, and love

Remember what I told you before
Jasmine means a Gift from God

I Lift up my hands and look up to the blue sky
When I saw rainbow colors smile into my eyes
Saying hello, hello, my dear, hello and then goodbye
I knew that time
Your soul, my dear
is happy and safe
In the hands of God
In the land of Uncle Sam
repeatedly I said
Thanks my God
Thanks my God
Keeping my sister safe
Full of energy and joyful life
Please my God
Please my God
Forever life
Forever life
keep my sister
Safe in the land of Uncle Sam

Beautiful Wisconsin

Mother's Nature is Calling Me

Thousand and thousands
of beautiful lakes
Green, Rock, Wazee
Devil's and Crystal lakes
merging and celebrating
the birth of a new spring day

Where a river is running smoothly
through a red place

Allium, Sedums, Russian sage
and Goldenrods flowers are everywhere
Butterflies with love and pride
fluttering around calling them
My friends, my friends
we are God's masterpiece of art
We are
We are God's masterpiece of art

Red chest, blue, and all colorful birds
Singing happily, the symphony of nature's play

I hear Ducks cheerfully:
Quack quack quack
Quack quack quack
Down to river or up to sky

Red-roof small farms spread here and there
Among green bluffs and wavy hills
Calling again for love and peace
For nature's love where man can give
The best of him, the best he can

Two wild brown Horses greeting me

With wide black eyes telling me:
The beautiful story about Wisconsin land
The wilder land of peace and love
The real wisdom of all man-time
Listen, my son; listen, my son
To the voice of love in your youthful soul
It will show your heart where you have to go

Golden Deer with their friendly elk
Playing with me my childhood game
The hiding game, as if I am still a little girl
Could not even blink for once.
My open eyes
Fearful of losing my joyful friends
In this game, the hiding game

Black and white cows coloring the farms
Inviting me for a tasteful cup
Cup of of their own tender love
A tasteful cup of golden milk
Cannot be found in any shop

Orange, red, and yellow leaves
Coloring the scene, the Autumn scene
the Autumn scene of Country Roads
The Country roads are up and down
K. P. V and rustic road
Cheering your soul with amazing scenes
Scenery of joy, Scenery of life

Bluff's Hiking trails are everywhere
Leading, at the end, to peaceful lakes
No matter what season of the year
You can always climb them with joyful friends

Mountain are here and mountain are there
It captures my eyes. The Cascade head[1]
White, white, white
Like a wedding veil
Shining on the head of a happy bride
Announcing soon the birth of new life
The birth of spring all around

How can I resist falling in love
Falling in love with this wilder land
The land of peace, mercy, and love
Wisconsin land, Wisconsin's land
Where God announces in all times
Love, mercy, and peace over this land

---

1. Cascade Head is the top of Cascade Mountain.

Handcuff of Eggs

She knocked my clinic's door
Early morning
Beautiful blond
As the sunshine of a summer's dawn
My American friend Suzan
With blue eyes
Happy joy
For what her hands carry
Of generosity and love
Greeting me with a white smile
Good morning, Fatema
Good morning
I lifted my head with a smile
In Arabic, I replied
صباح الخير عزيزتي
(Good morning, Dear)

I laughed and laughed
Seeing her opened, confused eyes
asking me the meaning of these vague words

When I answered her
She repeated
Saying that accent
Good morning
Without the point
On the letter H
We laughed together
To pronounce the words
How are you, Suzan
And how is it
She stretched her hands loaded
With handcuff of eggs
I honored her for her chickens

White, black, and blonde
Which was flirting with
all day and night times
This is for you dear
From my humble farm

That I loved so much
Only the farmer and the peasant
Know its depth
My pupils were amazed
From the generosity of my friend
Honesty and simplicity
Good case
Suddenly it jumped to mind
This question
Which we do not yet know an answer to
And still Scientists and decision-makers are puzzled
Suzan, you know who came first
Chicken or eggs
Suzan was lost in the question
For few minutes
Then she laughed
At the weirdness of the question I asked

She laughed and replied
I do not know the answer yet
But definitely
I care to fry eggs
In different shapes
And enjoy the breakfast
the beginning of my day

Probably the best
To ask this question
To experts and someone else

She left me with a head shake
With smile on the face
The doors open
At the end of day
I rushed to drive my car

Dreamy dinner
Then when I got home

I fried eggs
Dairy cow fattening
Dealt with
Syrian loaf of bread
With Cherry tomatoes, Green Onion, and Spicy salt

I prepared afterwards
A hot cup of tea

Thankfully, satisfied
Thus, gentlemen,
After saturating my empty gut
With fried Wisconsin farm eggs
With a loaf of Syrian bread
Grabs sight
The eye of the heart grew
Dreamy with a second egg handcuff
On the way to my gut again

Lilli

Her eyes are black
Like a fairy tale
A witch narrates
In the depth of night

White hair
As snowflakes
Adorned tree branches
On a silent winter night's feast
Illuminated by shimmering fireplace lights.

Pretty she is
Modest and soft
Kind and smart
With silky Mood

Easy to please
Modest request
loyal, beautiful
and generous friend

She has her own language
Could only be understood
by you or her special friends
The one who says
No need to translate
No need to prove
Her eyes express her feelings in a perfect way.

Confused how to please you
She dances around you
Left and right
Right and left
Forward and backward

Maybe she can
Cheer your face
With smile or hope.

She hugs you lovely
Comforts you kindly
From fear or pain
Jealous of you, no limit jealousy

She builds around your edges
Thinks she is protecting you
from humans' harms

She rubbed your feet
at the end of the day
Every now and then
She Looks at you
In love and longing
Bid you gentle massage
Relax your feet
From long-standing day
She kisses your forehead
Wishing you a happy dream

She does not belong
To the human world
Some people lost
Their human senses

She belongs to the world
Of love and real friendship
Where there is no existence for
hypocrisy and treachery of human race

Shereen and Domestic Viloence

Sherry came to me
Hopeless and depressed
Crying tears of oppression and despair

The palm of a usurper husband
Painted her left eye
Blue terrain (bruise)
Proof of manhood lost
Of compassion and love

This was not her first time
She faced betrayal
In the name of masculinity
and obedience of the husband and god

Sealing her life with him
With a deep wounded soul
cannot be healed forever life

Deception of customs and traditions
Marriage is the only security and support
For a woman or a girl in the Third World

She cried and cried and cried
Under the hits of her husband and mother-in-law
Without mercy or regrets
One girl, she lost
Surprising, she named her Mercy

She cried, cried, and cried
Complaining, torment of time
Between violence and betrayal
For her and two other children
The fruit of a relationship

The society named
Companionate marriage

Sherry echoed to me
Weeping relentlessly to
The hardest hearts
O my Lord, where is the salvation,
From prison, I thought
Initially
Orchard of basil, jasmine, and rose

She asked me what to do?
How to escape,
From an unjust husband and father
My angels, my other two children
The age of the buttons of roses
How to escape
From the looks of horror and fear
In the eyes of both of them
It haunts me even in my moments
Of sentiment and consciousness

Should I tell them the truth of the matter?
Or lie to them
What their eyes saw
was an illusion, delusion, or confusion?

I suffered a lot because of:
Motherhood
Femininity
Humanity

What to tell her
What do I do for a while?
Manhood has become

Unjust betrayal
Violence and exploitation

But God is in my soul
Is it nicer from
That God Who dwells in spirits
Echoed her on high
Do not let me down
Don't be silent
Never accept injustice and violence

A friend of yours
A real companion for a journey life
God indicated
I have created you
Free human beings
Silence about injustice
Demon destroys lives
Revolutionary rebel

Don't be afraid. Don't be afraid
Injustice is weaker
Justice is stronger
No matter how long

Don't be afraid, my sweetheart
I am with you
in the path of dignity
Path of joyful life

Report to the violence centers
Without hesitation, mercy, or regrets

It is the injustice of an innocent woman
To be a good wife

And a pure love

March to humiliation and weakness
No one will give you
If you stay with him
Dignity or respect or justice or love

Don't be afraid. Don't be afraid
For your beautiful angels
I feel your concern

God, be patient with
The oppressed winch
Of the oppressor gallows
Intransigent mighty

Hugged me and invited me
With words of appreciation and gratitude

Pray and ask God to grant me
Love, joy, and peace

Flying Out of Time

She was like a little girl
Enduring fun
Laugh, play
And swim tireless with the waves of life

She was dancing
And danced without boredom
Dance for her
Flying out of time

She was simply beautiful, kind,
educated with surprises of destiny and a culture of life

When meeting her for the first time
She attracted him by silky temper and gentle thoughts

He asked her, wondering,
"Why are you optimistic,
"Smiling and laughing,
"Without attention to time?"

She laughed.
"My happy childhood
"That gives me,
"An endless energy of joy.
"I never care for the passing of the time."

He declared to her after the passage of days,
"I love you, I love you
"As you are.
"I love you
"As the bird loves trees and as the sky loves rain
"As the sea loves the moon and as the stream loves the stone

"I love you, I love you, I love you."
As love never confessed any end or time

I apologized to him for laughing.
"Thank you, sir,
"But I do…
"I am not the one seeing my soul
"Flying with you
"I rarely see you
"Smiling or laughing
"Speaking of optimism,
"Or praising others.
"Who helped you?
"Even for the grace of the endowment.

"Since I've gotten to know you,
You're always
"comparing yourself with others
"Who have money
"power and power.

"So let's part.
"Perhaps you find what your soul seeking with time."
He replied confidently,
"I will change.
"I'll change with you

"With the passage of time.
"Your soul and mine will meet in the space of fun.

"I will change and change."
Until you say
Enough, enough
You achieved the goal

Because she is innocent
Honest and pure
Like the purity of water and rain
She believed him and agreed
To be together forever, life

It has not been days
And months with him.
The days revealed
What was hidden indeed
Shocks of life and destiny

She got sick, sick and sick
Her smile left her soul.
Feet stopped dancing with joy.

She steps aside
Wound and tears
Become her friends
His looks at her
Became blame and hate

She did not give up
Again and again
She gave him, over and over
Every chance to change
But every chance was ruined by his blame

She has been silent for years and years.
Suffering loneliness, fear and pain

Because she vowed commitments for faith

It slowly led to strangulation
Without guilt or reason, through her,

He was achieving his ambitions on her account
throwing his mistakes on her
Denying all what was given to him by her

And more than that,
Accusing her of lack of duty, passion and Love.

She asked herself over time
"Where did this anger, fake mask come from?

Misleading, narcissistic liar all that she finally found

Deceived, moment just came On time

"I have been plagued by illness of both your Thought and acts

"Life of sadness and bile.
"God will heal me
"From this affliction."

Forever decisive, the moment made her rise up
By lioness strength
To save the dignity of her life
From a male without manliness
No mercy, no conscience, no values or even regrets

She screamed with pain of Injustice and hurt

Enough is enough
Let us part now
I cannot tolerate
any more of this toxic life

No longer I can endure your blame, tantrums and hatred
That have no reason.

You killed all my feelings
I no longer care
For your false love.

Divorce for me is the only act
for gaining again my happy life

She left him and become again
a free bird
Laughing and dancing as it was
Beyond the limits of time.

Be careful, male, for what you seeded in female life
If it was injustice, hatred, or curse

You, over time,
Will pay the price
The worst price of
hatred and loss

For hurting woman
who gave all the best for a man when he was weak, ill, and sad

Your Words of apology
Or even kneeling, on your knees
Will not erase what harm you cause

She will return as she was.
Dance and fly
Out of time
And you will be
For the rest of your life
In the prison you built of
Lack of love

As Karma leaves no one.
What goes around comes around

Mistook the Address

They say that behind every great man there is a woman

And I say the most important reason for a woman's success in life is the father and the brother who respected her humanity and gave her all her rights and support in every step of her success.

I dedicate this poem to my father, on the occasion of Father's Day. May God bless him, my beloved Mustafa, and my brother Mahmoud, may God grant him a long life. They were behind much of the success that I achieved in my life and they are still.

He told her
I will make you, my beauty
The richest woman in the world
I decorate you with gold, diamonds and rose

I ride with you in the most luxurious cars
I dress you in the best brands
Fragrance you with the finest perfumes

I travel to all countries
Bestow on you wealth
Beyond reason

My beauty
I'm still awesome, guys
My family and my position
Needless to define
I have the best academic awards
From the best universities in this world

Women around the world chase me
Falling in love with me

By a hint from me
Without effort and torment

But I warn you
I have hard temper
Checkered fancy and mood
Quickly bored from women
Replace them as I change
Neck and shoe ties
Tough talk and even hurt
Sometimes to feel

I will never apologize, whatever it is
Wrong in position and speech
I want you to be prepared
To meet my requests
Anytime, anywhere

I am the man
I am the obedient commanded
My mother taught me that
Female function is to please the man
Whatever his requests, even if are hard

She said with calmness and respect
Are you done ,sir!!
From words!
He answered her with pride
Yes, and I allow you to respond
What befits the place

She laughed with delicacy
She asked him questions
Are you bored, sir?
Who is your mother?

Do you forget the previous talks?
Your neckties and shoes?
Do you think your fingers are the same ?!

Are you going to treat me the same way?!
If my passions and origin were Western
Live my life in contrast to our tradition
Free to do whatever I desire
Or will you give me lecture
The situation is different
Completely permissible
Having Western culture
It has privacy in customs and norms
So you and your mother and father
Will be my obedient server
To wipe and wash my dishes
Serve me my dinner and coffee every day
Massage my feet at the end of the evening

If I am from the East?
You will reverse standards, morals, and values
You and your family will treat me as servant
Humiliated, obedient servant
I have no right to declare my opinion or object !
My dignity will be wasted
No freedom of decision or suggest

Wonderful, sir!!
This duality of
Your standards and ethics
If there is room for morals!!

Are you still, sir?
After these questions
You think your fancy jewelry

education or wealth
Worthy for all women!!

Sorry, sorry, sir
I am one of the richest women
by my origin, scientific, and moral
I don't need men like you
You got the wrong address, sir
Greet your great mother
Honestly, without hypocrisy
She failed miserably
To raise you as a real man

Goodbye, sir
With all pleasure and peace
With my best wishes to you
To find what suits you life
My father and my brother
Gave me the reality
Beautiful and elegant
How to be manly, how to be a man

Goodbye, sir
As Nizar Qabbani described
The men in his poem Words
Words are not like words:
Construct a palace from illusion for me
I only live in it for a few moments
And I go back to my table
I have nothing but words
I entrust you with words
Not like words
You give it to a female
To express your position
Arrogant and shining

Your comment sinned, sir
For a lot of thought and evaluation
Not all of your fingers are the same

Sorry, sorry, sir
You mistook the address
Not all of your fingers are the same

I Declared My Defection

I declared my defection

I declared my defection from the women's tribe
Of a very special of women's tribe

No

Those who attack all women
And considers herself the best one, above all

She does not know the meaning of real love
There is no place in her heart to grant it

She looks as a chameleon
Change color according to Interests and goals

She poses her venom against Bachelorette, illiterate
widow, married, divorced
To the point that no one gets away from her harm

Show off that she has the best manners
The best couples, homes, and brands

Her children are the best ones
The children of others do not deserve appreciation, remembrance, or respect

If she knew her facts, the reality of the case.
She will discover that everything she brags about
It is a just fantasy and an illusion

Her main concern is people gossip
Whoever divorces, who is married, who dies
Whoever buys, whoever solds, Who borrowed

This is the face of a single female
Empty, trivial, shallow

Because she is jealous and envious
She could not keep
With miserliness, a companion, a neighbor, or even a friend

Everyone shaken off
Without greeting or saying goodbye

Like a spotted snake
Sting her nosebleed cramp
Near and far

She denies who stood by her side
At the time of sadness and distress

Rebels against who opened
The doors of his house
In times of misery and lack of luck

Even herself
no longer bear her injustice
Left alone
She gets lost in the darkness of a swindler

Her ability to destroy
Relationships, families, societies and even the world

O women and men
Close your doors
In the face of this kind of woman
Who causes
Badness and suffering
Depreciate her certificate of
Motherhood, education and ethics

Enough suffices
Our country until now
The consequences of ignorance, backwardness, and narcissism

Syria Syria

What a wonderful fairy tale I ever heard
Where all butterflies travel happily upon time
Between green mountain, pure rivers, and blue sky
Where azure sea and colorful hills have an endless love and life
Where love seeds planted in old time
Where beautiful flowers of humanity rise up in the sky
Where real love was only for the creator of this land

Syria Syria

I sense Rumi[1] and Tarbizi - Souls
Wondering and looking for each other
Between Aleppo and Damas
Whispering happily, lovers, lovers
Finally, we met in Syria, the holy land
Where our friendship is free of shame, sorrow, and harm
Where our souls rest until the end of time
Lovers, lovers whispering together
Syria is the land of peace, humanity, and love
Rising again above all this war of killing destruction and blood
Rising above all who said
Syria was ended before the end of the time
Rising again to the soul of God
Where love never misuses or causes harm

Colorful Butterflies met again and whispers with love
Dear, Dear God;
Your Love seeds are everywhere in the Syrian's land
Your Love wings flying high in the blue sky that covers The Syrian's land
With dignity, mercy, peace, and love

*Your Loving hands lifting kindly and happily the Syrian children in
your heart*

*Dear Dear God,
Bless me to be always
A butterfly in the Syrian's land*

*Dear Dear God
Thanks for being in the heart of the Syrian's land
Thanks for giving me the chance
To speak the Ugarit language, the language of all old time
Thanks for letting me fly freely in Damas[2]
The old inhibited city since man was found
Where church bells and mosque Azan play the wonderful symphony
of eternity and life*

*Dear Dear God;
Thanks Thanks again for giving me the chance
To hold the seeds of flowers, the seeds of love
So, I can still fly High in the sky of the Syrian's land
Where love plays the most beautiful music of any mankind*

---

1. Rumi : Jalal al- Din Rumi is a Persian poet, well known in the US, European and Middle East
2. Damas is Damascus

Mother of the Martyr

Her bitter wailing woke me up
From deep sleep at night
After a long hard day's work

She whispered in a painful quavering voice
Sorry, sorry, I am the mother of the martyr
I didn't mean to disturb or wake you up
From your quiet, slumbering night

I answered her and I was ashamed
Pangs of remorse
I was sleeping while she is still awake
Hoping and calling her martyr son
Perhaps he will wake up again
from his Eternal, Immaculate sleep

I could not fall asleep again
Hearing your sad voice
Moaning, my beloved one
Say what you want, dear

Our hearts are full with sadness
On your martyr's son
and on the death of every innocent man
by killers calling for disingenuous Arabic' Fall
Disguised as a freedom slogan
False, Misleading, Dedicated
Harvested Spirits and ruins
In the bleak Middle East
that suffered occupation in all forms
Throughout decades, times
Non read well, what history was hiding for him
between the lines of history, will be seen

She replied with deep sorrowful voice
And her beautiful green eyes
Pronounces dreams and dreams
About her son, that war chose
to be a martyr

What did he tell you ?!
What did he tell you ?!
Nostalgia and Longing killed me
To Hug my son
as I was doing repeatedly
at that time, near and far

I had sorrow until I lost
The joy of a comfortable life
it turns my night for day, my day for night
After the beloved's one died

What can I tell you about my vagrant soul?
In this universe that full of injustice
starvation and war
After I lost my beloved son
Despite the respect of people around
For martyr and martyrs
But Nobody can return my son to me,
even for a second
to hug him for the final goodbye

My friendly neighbor is also a martyr's mother
She visits me every now and then
Together, we remember that beautiful time
The time of our sons when they were young
They play war games
they choose
The role of the hero, traitor

martyr Or the loser,
the defeated, the winner

We did not realize then
this game was written
As the destiny of them long time ago
And that hit us all
From near and far
We cry sometimes and laugh sometimes
And we console one another sometimes
Hoping, we heal our deepest wounded hearts

We are fully aware
grief and sorrow and longing for them
became now our only friends

How do I calm her when she is the mother of the martyr
My words failed seeing her tears
I cried with her, I cried with her
For the Pain and sorrow on her face
She gently embraced me with kindness
patted on my tired shoulder with peace and love
from the burden of the war and the pain of destruction
And human starvation from a traitorous siege
Despicable oppressor the heart yearning for
My homeland that injured the sufferer
Swallow it up, the fangs of greed
Molars of oil monsters and bandits
the new wealth owners have no morals no mercy on the land they
were born

Why are you crying, Fatema ??
you have not lost a son as a martyr!!

I am crying for every one

is at the age of spring and amber
The beans, basil, and jasmine
Who was killed in this crazy war
The refugee cried trying to escape
On the deck of insecure boat
the price was paid in advance by
War, asylum and displacement gangs
The boat overburdened its passengers
Whereby were drowned
Or swim, trying to reach safety land
Or a dead person carelessly, unidentified
On the shores of immigration and westernization
Or persecuted by a female or male journalist
who lost their humanity in a fit
Hatred, anger, and threat

I cry for every martyr
Who died under destruction, bombing, or want

Although Jibran Khalil Jibran
Taught me to hold
My cold hands with my warm hands
May it heal my ailing heart
However, she was unable to heal my soul
From the effects of this war
In the heart, mind, and soul

You see my dear
That we are all as one
One way or another
We became the mother of the martyr

Because the blood of the martyr is priceless
He waters our land with generosity and wondrous
Wheat spikes, Cotton, and jasmine will grow up again

we will harvest bread and clothing as well a fragrant essence
the perfume of martyrdom and martyr
Will let us hope again, my dear
For the sake of every martyr's thoughts
Whoever wishes for us
prosperity , peace and love
Smiled, with a smile of victory and liberation
For our children to live peacefully in a world
Free of destruction or war

Remember, remember, my dear
From the womb of sorrows
Is born the joys of a beloved homeland
From the blood of the martyrs' blooms
The bean, basil, and jasmine
Amber grow
In every mountain, valley and plain

The mother of the martyr will remain
an example, front line, and lighthouse
For mothers of the new generation
Let the heads bent, and the hats are lifted
Respect for the mothers of the martyr and for each martyr

Wheat Spikes

In my country they kill
elderly, children, and women
In the name of equality, freedom, and democracy

The number of soul martyrs become sadly parallel to bodies' martyrs

In my homeland, they destroyed the ruins
On the pretext that they are idols
So the ruin's stones became the witness Of the invader brutality

In my country, they burned wheat spikes
Until her ashes became a reflection
Of Malice and hatred
The unjust rapist invader

The elderly
The farmer cried
On wheat spikes
Water it with tenderness, generosity, and love
Perhaps, its harvest is enough
From needs, and treachery of time

In my country, the birds
Sing sad about what has become
The sky is overcast
With clouds of anger and revenge

The Mediterranean Sea is rough from
Injustice and treachery of time

Youssef cries deeply and complains to his father again what his brothers did.
During the years, years of destruction, poverty and war

In my country, church bells ring
Grief for the martyrs and the poor
The minarets of mosques ring, announce a prayer
For wheat germs, it may germinate again

The hope revives the souls of the sleepers
Fairness to humans, stone, and man
Apologizes for the spikes of wheat were burned

So, O man
O man

Where is humanity!!!
Where is humanity!!!
where is human rights!!!

As history has proven
Over time
The day of the oppressor's punishment
Is inevitable and soon will be announced
No imperialism lasted
Neither kingdom, neither occupation, neither the most powerful man

The Bread Loaf

When poverty begins to play its music on the strings of life, all voices will be silent in respect of the testimony of the poor. And at that moment, the homelands become all strangers. Real poverty remains the poverty of values and morals. Let us all fight against the moral poverty that comes from the corruption of conditions.

Hey, dear Gentlemen

Once upon a time
A judge claimed the honor
Justice and equality

Throw people behind prison walls
For theft and wasting public money

His first trial
Was for the poor man
The echo came up loud:
Court
Then the investigation began

The most important question
In a furious roaring voice
From a conceited judge
To a poor accused
Covered his face with grief and pain
Speak out
You fraudster thief
Why did you steal a loaf of bread???
You know that it is forbidden!!!
You will be held accountable!!!
In front of the public and mankind

The poor cried because of the lack of the money
He answered, "Sir,
I am neither a thief nor a fraud
Poverty forced me to act.
What does not satisfy the soul and mind
To feed my hungry children, fearfully of death and Loss .

The judge marveled
And surprised, most surprisingly
From the response of the poor-man.
And his justification for the bread loaf
He insisted on saying it
What the poor did was stealing and forbidden.

The poor could not conceal
Surprised, tougher amazement
He lost his temper and started screaming:
Why did you leave the rich thieves?
They blow public money
Why you do not hold them accountable
As you did to me
In the name of justice and equality
Panting behind me
As monsters are panting
Behind prey in the open
Thus relieving me and others
From the status of poverty
Thus preventing theft
And wasting public money

The judge rushed from his seat angry and mad
To attack the poor man
Humiliation and understanding
He immediately asked to throw him
Behind the prison bars

Neither one heard

Thus, dear gentlemen
You can realize
From where come
Society and nation corruption.
Inevitably, it comes from the corruption of morals
On the top of the head, corruption of the judiciary

Thank you
You and we stay happy
Far from such a judiciary

Stop Attacking

Thanks for Emoji Bag
Filled with a few dollars
One of the readers sent it to me

They attacked me for saying
America is my second homeland
Precious on thought and conscience
A country taught me how to convert
The wound to rule and joys

You inspired me, dear
This bunch of dollars
On my written words
With respect and gratitude
For a homeland that hosted me
With love and respect

Enough is enough, O man
Attacking peoples and homelands
Stop stigmatizing people
Didn't you know, human?
God created us people and nations
Without borders, passports, or fences
To get to know each other with kindness
We exchange the best for us and for generations

So why do you attack your human brother?!
Otherwise, you would be alone in the open!!
Suffering from loneliness, pain, and abandonment!!

Have you not heard beloved Lebanon (Marcel Khalife)?
Tweet in the space of Uncle Sam's land
His song that represented every human being;
Gentlemen, masters of the prophets

Do not ask the trees for its name
Do not ask valleys about her mother
From my front Luminance Sword has defected
And from my hand stems River's water
All people's hearts are my nationality
cancel my passport from me
Cancel the borders and fences
I was and still am that human
Who remotely invokes his human brother

Despite the oceans and seas
Which separated me from him
Borders and fences
What this human was
Only the English national (John Lennon)
Forget passion and heart
We have always been blown away by his righteous voice
Across the planet and the homelands;
Imagine, Imagine, Imagine
There are no homelands
Nothing is worth
Murder, death, or destruction
Imagine that there are no religions
Imagine that all human beings live in peace

You may accuse me of delirium
But I am not the only one who wishes
To join us one day to the human world
The whole world becomes one beautiful home
Free from displacement, hunger, and diseases

I will not back down, I will not back down, I will not back down
To extend my hands to you,
O man
Oh, who attacked me

A handful of dollars
doubted my belonging, my loyalty
To my home country, Syria
The cradle of civilization and man

I forgave you; I forgive you, human
For attacking me
A handful of dollars
Because I am more sad and pained than you
For what happened to my country
from killing, displacement, and destruction
Because I am fully aware
To attack me
that came from anger, sadness, and frustration
For the ruin of my country and your country

But excuse me, excuse me
Excuse me, human
I will never apologize to you
for considering America my precious homeland
A huge ton on my heart
Precious thought and emotions
Because of the hearts of all people
Was and still is my nationality
I belong to her proudly
Eliminate the borders and fences

Let the people live in freedom and peace
In a world rich in music, sciences, and arts

Thank you, human
Oh, who attacked me
For a handful of dollars
I have inspired my pen
To write these words

In fairness to all people and nations

Remember, always remember, human
Before you send me a second
Emoji, a bunch of dollars
You are totally impotent
to smear my dignity
Or change what is in my heart
Of love and gratitude
For all people and homelands
For the hearts of all people
It was and still is my nationality
To which I belong proudly
Let the borders and fences fall
Long live peoples and homelands

FROM THE AUTHOR

Life is an unpredictable journey to a joyful eternity.

We think the world is the place we were born and grew up, but the real world is you and me. It is Mother Nature who is calling us all desperately: for humanity, for love, peace, and mercy.

In this world, a world full of poverty, war, hunger, and

destruction we are all searching for our real identities. Our real Identity is our humanity, and humanity cannot be achieved without transforming our souls to authentic souls.

We think we will be happy when everything Is perfect in our lives, but we learn from painful experiences we are going through to have faith in the Creator, in God. Be grateful and happy, then our lives will be in the right path.

They call nature Mother Nature, so woman, never ever underestimate yourself and your strength, because as they always say, nature is a mother and you are this wonderful strong beautiful nature.

Painful experience wounded us at the beginning, but then it taught us the best lesson we can have in life: to move on. Focus on presence. Hope for the best. It teaches us how to turn our pain to joy and our weakness to strength.

Never ever give up your rights. Do not let anyone steal your freedom and happiness.

Forget the painful past, enjoy the present, and always stay positive that the best is yet to come.

Happiness is a personal choice. Make it your choice, and always remember the best is yet to come.

Yes, the best is yet to come.

Milton Keynes UK
Ingram Content Group UK Ltd.
UKHW020607050124
435502UK00010B/81